TRUE HAPPINESS

Key Secrets To Be Happy And Healthy With Positive Thinking

MARYAM LOUIS

TABLE OF CONTENTS

INTRODUCTION

The main factor affecting how well life is lived is happiness. Have you ever come across someone who drives an ancient car and lives in a modest house? Although they may not be materially wealthy, their pleasure is beyond affluent.

Life presents us with challenges that we all wish we could avoid. This may alter our mood and perspective. However, you have the option of choosing to be happy or miserable throughout your life. The only person who can control it is you. Even if there are many aspects of life that you cannot control, your happiness should never depend on another person.

We live in a world that frequently encourages us to redeem ourselves with material items, which is one of the biggest obstacles to true pleasure. Then we contrast what we possess with what those around us possess. We might feel inferior to them if they have more than we do. This has a significant impact on one's degree of happiness.

Being overly busy might also lead to happiness being neglected. You cannot enjoy life and have time for yourself if you are constantly working and running errands. Remain calm and concentrate on your most important priorities. There is no justification for working nonstop or doing everything on your own.

True happiness requires communication to happen. They won't know what you want or what you won't put up with if you don't tell them. Never feel bad about setting certain boundaries in relationships so that you can be happy.

You need to consider what happiness means to you in order to be truly happy. What it means to you might not mean the same thing to the person next to you. Once you've determined what it is, you can concentrate on enhancing your time management, communication, and ability to adapt so that you can actually attain it. Make sure you are not your own worst enemy since perceptions might prevent you from experiencing happiness.

You can argue that there isn't much you can do to improve the unpleasant folks in your vicinity. While to some extent that is true, you cannot allow their negativity to bring you to their level. You must be content with the reflection of yourself and the person you see yourself to be.

While being content most of the time is conceivable, being content all the time is not. Additionally, you can use your joy to get through the most trying circumstances in your life. It's possible that as you read through these martials, you'll spot some obstacles that have been getting in your way.

With the help of concepts and ideas that you can incorporate into your daily activities, you can also feel empowered. By doing this, they'll quickly assume the form of automatic daily behaviours that you'll develop.

When it comes to your happiness, it's crucial to be in control. You can't just wait around and expect it to happen. Weeks, months, and years follow the days! Do you want to spend them experiencing life to the fullest or do you want to spend them feeling the same as you do now?

Your general view on life has a lot to do with how happy you are. You don't need to have the biggest or greatest automobile or house on the street. You don't have to run a business as the CEO. True happiness might be hampered if your life is defined by financial possessions.

Your happiness is also influenced by the nature of your connections with your family, friends, coworkers, and other people in general. It's time to examine those connections closely and determine how reflective they are. You should feel secure and content in your relationships. You need to alter them if you frequently experience anxiety, sadness, or anger around them.

According to studies, those who are happy generally perform better in all aspects of their lives. They are less prone to illness. They typically experience fewer difficulties having kids or getting divorced. Additionally, they often perform better at work because their employer observes that they appear happy to be there.

You can alter your life in a way that makes you happier right now. It makes no difference where you reside, how much money you make, or your age. It's never too late to be joyful and truly appreciate life. These happiness tips and

tricks can put you on the right track to realising
your goals.

Chapter 1

POSITIVE THINKING

Negative thoughts can make us perceive difficulties that don't really exist around us. Negativity might cause us to worry and destroy our happiness. The difficulty unfortunately is that many people don't know just how negative they have become. It may be such a habit that people are unaware of it.

Another element of the problem is that you may be around people that are negative all the time. They can zap your energy if you aren't careful. You are going to need to make some modifications around those types of people to help you move forward and be happy. We shall discuss that more in the future chapter.

You may be saying that you can't help who you are working with. Maybe the person at the desk immediately next to you does nothing but whine. It can reduce you from a smiling, joyful person in the morning to being grouchy and wishing it was time to go home.

You can't change other people and how they think, but you can decrease how you let it affect you. When negativity is around, it seems to damage the entire surrounding atmosphere. You can let it continue to do so or you can make it better and be happy in spite of what others think.

One of the easiest and most effective methods to convince people to stop being so negative is to ask them how they can fix it. For example, if you are listening to someone moan about another person, remind them respectfully that they need to talk to that person about it if it is ever going to get better.

If someone is saying they don't comprehend a school task, remind them they need to talk to the instructor about it. When there is a complaint about something, ask what they can do to make it better. All of these alternatives are fairly straightforward on your end. Yet it will stop those nasty folks in their tracks. They will cease being like that around you.

<u>Optimistic</u>

Pay close attention to how you react to things. If you feel that you are negative with them, shift things around. Focus on being optimistic so that you can feel cheerful. You may be astonished at first as you realise the number of times negative thoughts come into your mind.

However, the idea is going to be to convert them into something positive every single time. You will realise over time you are having negative thoughts less frequently. You will also realise that you fall into the habit of automatically being positive. In time, it will become a significant part of who you are and your lookout for life.

Count Your Blessings

When you start to get upset, think of all of the blessings you have in your life. Take a moment each morning to add up the little things that will offer you joy that day. Maybe you will get to meet someone new for a date that evening. Perhaps you are going to eat lunch with an old acquaintance.

Before you go to bed at night, think about the small and big things that occurred that made your day a wonderful one. Did you obtain some free time to read a book you enjoyed? Were you able to take the dog out for a walk and some time to play at the park? These are the little things in life that really do make us happy!

Be Grateful

If your style of thinking is about what you desire and what you didn't get, you will always be disappointed. When your perspective is one that allows you to feel appreciative then you can get through the bad times. You will also be joyful because you realise the contentment that comes from the simple things in your life.

Be Kind

Smiling is one of the best methods to feel happy than you do right now. When you smile, others will grin back at you. They are going to see you as someone that they can approach. They will feel comfortable around. Being kind isn't hard, it is a choice.

Hold the door open for someone instead than rushing on to take care of your business. Allow someone else to go first at a four way stop when no one is sure who should go next.

Most essential, be gentle to yourself. Think of all of the positive ways that you have done well at work, at home, and for others that day. Don't dwell on the things that didn't go your way or the to do list that never seems to finish.

Doors Open And Close

Life may not always go according to your plans. Perhaps you applied for a job you truly wanted and didn't get hired. However, that indicates that another door is going to open for you. Don't close your eyes to this or you may miss out on the best things that are likely to come along.

Always search for the good in any situation. No matter how awful it may appear, there is always something to be glad about. When you look at things from such a point of view, you will be mentally empowered. You will know that regardless of what life tosses your path, you are going to be able to overcome it. When you look at life from such a standpoint, you will also enjoy the wonderful things when they do happen in your life.

Envision

By closing your eyes, you can spend some time imagining what it takes to make you happy.

Focusing on the outcome that will develop is a terrific approach to start your day off well. It can also be a lovely method to go off to sleep at night. When you picture what you genuinely desire, you may help to make it happen.

During these visualising events, think about how you FEEL during them. Are you happy? Why are you happy? That is what you should be focusing on. It could be due to where you are or who you are with that makes all the difference to you.

Don't Fear Mistakes

Everyone makes mistakes, so don't think you are the only one. If you don't take some risks now and again, you aren't going to make mistakes. Yet you aren't going to get that degree of bliss you want either. Put yourself out there and you may be harmed, but you may also receive the finest possible circumstance.

If you don't take the risk, you will remain frozen precisely where you are. You will also wind up with regrets surrounding "what if" and those are the kind that can take away your happiness.

This doesn't imply you act irresponsibly and then blow off the fact that a mistake was made. Instead, it means you do your utmost best. It signifies you learn from your mistakes and continue to keep your head up high. It also means you have the self-worth of knowing you gave it your all.

Chapter 2

SURROUND YOURSELF WITH GOOD PEOPLE

If you spend time among cheerful people, you are likely to be happy too. There will be significantly less negativity in your life. There are plenty of things you can do to guarantee you have strong relationships. Too often, people attempt to have as many friends as possible. They cherish the thought that people like them.

As the expression goes, it is better to have 4 quarters than 100 cents. Simply said, it is the quality of the company you keep that matters, not the volume of it. Surround yourself with folks who you love, that you trust, and that you feel comfortable around. You should be able to chat to them and feel like they support you.

Communication

One of the things that will help you with developing healthier relationships is improved communication. Listen more than you talk and you will be astonished at how you feel. We are all distinct with different points of view. We aren't going to agree with those we love all the time, but we can be respectful of those differences too.

Don't make assumptions or allow misconceptions to hinder your connections. Be open and honest about who you are and what you desire.

Tell the truth, even when it is difficult and you will be a happier person. You won't be burdened with remorse or worry that the truth will one day come out.

Get To Know People

Don't hesitate to get to know new individuals. You can do so through your children's activities, your hobbies, or just spending time wandering about your area. Be a part of what goes on in your neighbourhood and you will be able to meet people. If you observe someone at work who is positive and seems like a wonderful person, take the time to get to know them.

Make An Effort

Relationships need time to develop. Don't be in a rush to go from just meeting to anything very in depth. Give the relationship time to grow and to bloom. Don't be a wallflower who waits for people to approach them. Make an effort to smile and to be friendly.

People aren't always going to remember what you say to them. With that in mind, don't spend too much time being nervous about what to say. What people will remember is how you made them feel. If you make an effort to show people that you are fun, cheerful, and joyful, then they will be pulled to you like a magnet.

Personal Contact Is Important

While social media is exciting, it has transformed the way that people communicate. Being joyful still involves some personal contact. While sending an email or a text is straightforward and convenient, don't rely on it all the time. Pick up the phone and call someone so you can hear their voice.

Send someone a handwritten thank you note and it will definitely brighten up their day. Schedule time to eat lunch with a friend or to take a walk at the park with someone so you can get caught up. You will be happy if you are keeping that human interaction in your regular routine.

Ask For Help

There will be instances when life isn't what we had planned. When you find yourself in a difficult circumstance, ask for support. You may count on friends and family to get you through those hard spots. They may have solutions that you didn't think about. They can also provide you encouragement along the route to help you stay positive.

If you think you have to carry the weight of the world on your shoulders, you don't. Nothing will drive you to feel depressed, exhausted, and like there is no hope as being on your own and isolated during terrible times can. No one can travel that journey for you, but they can be there to walk right along with you.

<u>Give Help</u>

Be a good friend and family member too. Don't only contact people when you need aid. Be eager to reciprocate by offering your support when they ask for it. Depending on the circumstances, you may be able to offer your help or do something helpful for them without even being asked.

<u>Cut Out Negative People</u>

One of the hardest elements of being happy by surrounding oneself with nice people is letting go. Just because someone has been in your life for a long time doesn't imply they deserve to remain there. If you are involved in intimate relationships, you have friends or family, or you just sense that someone is taking advantage then you need to sever those ties.

It can be really difficult to do, but it is going to be a step towards happiness that you will be quite proud you have taken. With family, it can be hard to entirely block them out. You can start to distance yourself though and set some ground rules. The same is true of co-workers that you don't believe you have a quality relationship with.

Counselling

If you have a hard time developing great relationships, you may need to seek some professional help. Through counselling, you can uncover limitations that could be blocking you from actual satisfaction in relationships. Perhaps there are trust concerns or other aspects that you aren't entirely aware of.

Chapter 3

LEARN TO SAY NO

There has to be balance in your life for you to be happy. We all have the same amount of time in a day for work and for other things. If your schedule is too complete, you aren't going to be happy. Yet you may feel like you have to say yes to everything that comes your direction.

Learning to say no is going to make you much happier! It can take some effort, but the trick is to make sure you don't let guilt get to you. This doesn't imply you never pitch in and help with anything. However, it implies that you carve out time for rest, for fun, and for your other responsibilities.

Take Part In Activities That Mean Something To You

When you are requested to take part in an event, think about how you will feel about it. If the activity is something that is meaningful to you, then help with it. For example, if you are requested to help with a fundraising for the community that could be near to your heart.

When the activity is something you are interested in, you will be driven to continue with it. You will also get a great lot of personal gratification from how you have contributed to that cause. Doing so is going to help you. I feel extremely happy.

<u>Daily Planner</u>

One method to reclaim your time back is to develop a daily calendar. Mark out portions of time on that planner each day. Unless an emergency comes along, don't feel that time up with anything else. If you are asked to help with something that you truly don't want to commit to due to a lack of time or other reasons, speak up.

<u>No Explanation Necessary</u>

The most prevalent reason why people don't say no is that they don't have a good justification. Those that are asking can be quite good at getting folks to say yes. For example, they may make you feel terrible that you aren't going to take part in what they are asking.

Others will try to impress you in order to get you to reply that you will do so. For example, they may state that you are very creative and that is why they would like you to be in charge of marketing for the fundraiser.

You don't have to give a reason when it comes to saying no. Say it gently, thank them for asking you, and then stand firm with your no reply. You don't have to give any reason at all about why you can't take part in what they are asking.

People Pleaser Mentality

Part of the reason it is harder to say no is that we tend to have a people pleasing mentality. We want people to like us, and we often feel answering yes will encourage that. It may in some cases, but you have to draw a line. If you are being tugged in all directions, you aren't going to be happy.

You aren't going to be able to dedicate enough time for relaxation, for work, and for all of your commitments. Instead, you become resentful of what you have committed to. You may do it, but you aren't going to be enjoying it. Instead, you have a chip on your shoulder. When that project is done, you sense relief rather than personal satisfaction.

Be Clear

Don't be evasive about why you are saying no. Don't give them any sense that you are thinking about it or that you may cave in. Simply mention that you are already taking on too much and you have made a vow to yourself not to take on anything new right now.

They should have enough respect for you to take that as a final no. If someone tries to continue to persist, they should fall into the category of persons you need to think about eliminating out of your life. They can sap your vitality and hinder you from being as happy as you could be.

Chapter 4

MAKE TIME FOR YOU

Free up time in your daily life especially for you. It can be time for you to enjoy your coffee on the porch or to read a couple chapters in a book. Never feel bad for making time simply for you. There may be several roles you perform including husband, parent, and employee.

However, that doesn't mean you should lose sight of your own wants and your own desires. When that happens, you may start to feel robotic in what you do and what actions you take. You may not feel like you are fulfilling your full potential.

Trust Your Instincts

When it comes to doing what makes you happy, go with your instincts. As long as what you do doesn't injure others or hurt your general well-being, then take part in it. I have always appreciated live music, so I go to plenty of concerts. Many people think that I am too old for that or that I should preserve my money.

Yet it is what makes me really happy. For those short hours, nothing else matters. I can let go of stress, not worry about problems at home, and just enjoy the concert. I have also made some fantastic friends that share the same love of music. Some of them I get to meet regularly.

Others, I only get to see at a concert so it is even more wonderful when I do spend time with them. You know better than anyone else what it is that will make you happy. Think about how you would feel if you didn't take part in those activities. If removing them will diminish your degree of happiness, then keep taking part in them. Not everyone will understand that, but spending that time on what you enjoy is for you - not for them.

Own Who You Are

Don't make excuses for spending time on what you enjoy doing. Own who you are and what you enjoy. Your personality should reflect what you like spending time doing. Men seem to have a tougher difficulty than women with this, especially if what they enjoy doing isn't necessarily considered as masculine.

For example, I once worked with a guy who adored baking. He loves to test different cuisines in his spare time. Yet he was quite shy to tell others what he liked to do. When he would bring sweets to the office, folks would comment that he was a lucky guy that his wife produced such nice foods for him.

He didn't disclose with many of us that he was actually the one performing the baking. Only those that he genuinely trusted not to tease him about it. In a facility that was largely guys, you can imagine how he imagined they may react to the fact that he was their boss yet at home baking in the evenings.

It can be challenging at times to be true to who you are and not hide your habits or hobbies. Your personality is distinct nevertheless and you should be proud of it. By taking time for yourself to enjoy what you like, you will become more comfortable in your own skin.

Don't apologise to others if your route is one that is different from theirs. One of the cornerstones for quality relationships is not only accepting what you have in common with someone but also respecting the differences.

If you aren't accepting of yourself and what you provide, how can you expect anyone else to be? Learning to appreciate yourself and to be kind to yourself is a significant step towards happiness. If you can't enjoy spending time alone with you, why would anyone else want to?

Reflect

When you spend time alone, you may relax and you can ponder. Think about some pleasant recollections that you have. They will put you in a pleasant mood and enable you to feel content. Think of problems you have worked to overcome, and be proud of the steps you made to achieve positive improvements. You might also think about the future and how you plan to reach the goals you have in place.

The process of contemplation allows us to slow down and to be in touch with ourselves. We may live a very fast paced life, and that means that we don't always obtain the results we are hoping for. We can develop tunnel vision and reflection allows you to actually view the big picture.

Give Your Time

Even though you are creating time for yourself, do what you can to volunteer some time now and then. If you enjoy knitting, make some extra hats and scarves that you may donate to a homeless shelter. If you enjoy baking, take some cookies over to the local senior centre for them to enjoy.

Go through your home and take out clothing and other items you no longer use. There is always someone who can use them. Donate them to a shelter or a second hand store. Do everything you can to give back with part of your free time.

Hobbies

Find a few pastimes you really enjoy. If you aren't sure, try something new. Perhaps a dance class or an art class. You can also spend some time organising a reading club or you can perform some house maintenance chores. Your interests should represent who you are and what you like taking part in.

They can help you relieve tension and to feel like you are completing something positive. A couple of hobbies can keep you from being bored or taking part in activities that are undesirable.

Chapter 5

GET YOUR FINANCES UNDER CONTROL

One of the key elements in life that can steal your happiness is financial stress. It is true that the economy is bad, but that isn't an excuse to be on bills and owning heaps of debt. Take responsibility so that you are able to feel good about your financial status.

If you hold the idea that more money would fix your troubles, you are wrong. It is true that you should aim to live above the poverty level. Yet financial comfort isn't going to correlate to more happiness. For many folks, it can mean less free time and increased stress.

Love Your Career

The number of hours and years that the average person spends working in their lifetime is relatively high. Therefore, you need to enjoy your career if you are going to be happy. Don't pursue a career you despise only to make more money.

Of course it is crucial to make sure you have a job that will pay the expenses!

Some people get a job and they stay with it for decades. They continue to advance up the ladder and they do really well. There are jobs that are a good beginning point, but they aren't going to move ahead. Don't get locked in a dead end job. It is never too late to increase your knowledge. Look for a new employment, learn a new skill, or even go back to college to earn a degree.

Budgeting

In order to get your finances under control, you need to conduct a careful inventory of your spending. Make a list of all of your monthly bills. This should include:

- Rent/Mortgage
- Car Payments/Leasing/Public Transportation
- Insurance
- Utilities
- Groceries
- Medical supplies/Medications
- Childcare

Next, develop a list of all of your variable expenses. These are unsecured debt items that you can pay off. This should include:

- Credit Cards
- Personal Loans
- Revolving Credit

Make a note of all of your revenue and compare it to your spending. This is what you have left over each month. With your variable expenses, do what you can to pay more than the minimum each month so you pay it off quicker and lower overall interest.

Plan Of Action

If your budget appears out of control, get help. There are several financial companies that will aid you to budget without any price. They have budgeting seminars that allow you to get back on track. If you have a significant other, the plan of action for finances should be done as a team. Create targets that you both work towards and re-evaluate your plan often.

If your spending is significantly more than your income, it is time to make some changes. Can you find a second job to boost the income and pay down debt? Can you work from home in your free time to earn additional money for the household? Perhaps you need to move to a lesser priced property or you need to trade in your car for one that is more economical.

If you owe a considerable amount of unsecured debt, talk to them about lowering your interest or a payback. If you offer a lump sum of cash for the account they may drastically lessen the dollar amount that you owe in order to successfully eliminate that debt.

It is advised to avoid consolidation lenders as they frequently have large costs and your credit score can suffer in the end. You also want to avoid filing bankruptcy unless it is really essential.

<u>Extras</u>

Pay attention to how much you spend for extras. Eating out, going to the movies, and even buying coffee at a café can all add up rapidly. When you determine where you are spending your money, you can cut down on some of those expenditures. Identify one or two items you truly wish to have extra. Allocate an allowance for them and once it is spent, that is it.

<u>Savings</u>

In addition to paying your monthly payments, you should also be paying yourself. Allocate a portion of your salary or a specific monetary amount for savings. This is necessary so that you can have money in place for emergencies. Then you won't have to use a credit card or revolving credit should there be an emergency. When you use money you have saved, you don't have that interest to think about.

<u>Retirement</u>

Preparing for the future is also very important. Retirement may seem like a long time from now, but it will arrive. Being prepared for it is incredibly crucial and you need to start as early as you can.

If your employer has retirement programmes such as 401k, donate the maximum that you can. If your employer doesn't offer this, you should talk to a retirement advisor. They can help you to get accounts set up. If you go from one job to the next, roll over your retirement plan instead of cashing it out.

You should diversify your portfolio so that you have retirement assets spread around. This can assist you to avoid a huge loss should any certain investment not do very well. The level of risk you accept with your retirement is equally crucial to think about. The closer you get to retirement, the less risk you should be with those funds.

Chapter 6

OFFER FORGIVENESS

Forgiveness is a very potent source of happiness. We can cling onto grudges and blunders for far too long. They can poison our mind, our soul, and take away from the beautiful things in our lives. When we fail to forgive, resentment might get the best of us.

When we talk about forgiving in order to promote happiness, there are 3 categories:

- Asking for forgiveness

- Offering forgiveness

- Forgiving yourself

Asking for Forgiveness

There can be various reasons why we don't beg for forgiveness. Maybe we have too much pride or we believe that too much time has gone by. Maybe we worry that it won't matter to the other person or persons involved and it will be a lost cause. Asking for forgiveness is never a show of weakness.

Instead, it suggests that you desire to release those unwanted feelings once and for all. You can ask for forgiveness in person or you can write a personal letter. A phone call can be good too but if you aren't sure how the other side would reply. It may be best not to.

You can always send them a letter and tell them you would want to talk and then they have the opportunity to contact you if they would like to. A phone call or in person can put them on the spot and make it hard for them to come to terms with their feelings due to you contacting them.

With a letter it can offer them some time to think about all of it and to make the decision to listen to what you have to say. Make sure your request for forgiveness is genuine and that it specifically says what you are apologising for. You don't have to assign blame and you don't have to delve into the specifics of who was right or wrong.

Even if they don't accept your apology, you will have the peace of mind that you extended the olive branch. You will be able to let go of the issue and you will know that you did what you could to put things right. The happiness that it would provide you is tremendous because you will be able to let go.

Offering Forgiveness

When it comes to offering forgiveness, strive to be compassionate. Keep in mind how tough it can be difficult for someone to reach out to you. If you sense they are sincerely remorseful for what happened, then let it go. You may have some questions that you would like them to answer. It is fine to inquire so that you can obtain some closure with the incident.

It isn't always instant that you will be able to offer forgiveness. It is appropriate to tell someone that you are no longer furious but that you are wounded. Your emotions can shift before you can totally let go and forgive. You may realise that you can no longer let the relationship go back to what it used to be, but that you have some respect for that person today.

One of the hardest things to do in terms of granting forgiveness so that you can be happy is to let go when there is no apology. We have to remember that people do things for a number of reasons. Perceptions can have a major impact on what hurts us or makes us furious.

Sometimes, we are harmed in the crossfire of what someone else is going through. They may be battling with addictions, mental health, or other concerns that we aren't entirely aware of. Try to be kind and to forgive when you can. This doesn't mean they win, it just means you are no longer willing to keep rehearsing that situation in your head and letting it get the best of you.

Forgiving Yourself

We can be our own worst critics, and that implies that we can destroy our own happiness. You have to be forgiving with yourself. Let go of previous mistakes and move on. Tell yourself that you did the best you could with the facts you had at the time.

The fact that you are able to see today that there was a better way to approach anything implies that you have evolved. You aren't making the same mistakes again and again and not making positive improvements in your life.

In life, if you keep staring in that rear view mirror, you will miss what is in front of you. Your past may have left some scars, but they simply prove that you were stronger than what was trying to keep you back. That is surely something to smile about!

<u>Counselling</u>

Sometimes, the challenges that have transpired are just too enormous for us to work out on our own. If you can't forgive, you aren't alone and you shouldn't feel terrible about it. Give it time to work through emotions and to see a brighter side of things. Talking to a counsellor can be a good approach to deal through feelings.

It can aid in the healing process so that you can move on and so that you can feel happy. Forgiveness doesn't mean that you no longer feel hurt or angry. It simply means you are in control over those feelings and you are empowered by your dedication to be joyful in spite of what has occurred in the past.

Chapter 7

STOP COMPARING YOURSELF TO OTHERS

If you tend to think that the grass is always greener on the other side, you are diminishing your own enjoyment. It can be difficult at times to be happy for the success of others. However, that often has to do with a lack of self respect and a lack of being pleased with what you have accomplished.

Keep in mind that you don't know the battles they have endured to get where they are today. Very few people achieved it without sacrifice, hard labour, or without blunders along that way. What you see is them at the top of the mountain, but often you miss that long climb to reach the peak.

Appreciate

Take some time to genuinely enjoy what you have around you. If you are able to make ends meet, you have some great relationships, and you love your activities then you are doing well.

It is acceptable to have objectives and to aim for more. Just make sure you don't miss out on the enjoyment right in front of you due to reaching and reaching.

Jobs

It can be frustrating to work with someone day in and day out that has a stronger job in the business than you do. Perhaps you applied for that same position when it came open and you didn't get it. Find reasons to be quite content in the job you do have. Stop and contemplate how many unemployed individuals would love to have your job if it was offered to them!

If you aren't content with your job, think about making some adjustments. Perhaps you can learn a new area of the business you already work for. Maybe it is time to take on a new journey at another firm. You aren't bound down to the employment you have unless you have a contract for a specified period of time. A fresh start, new faces, and new challenges can be just what you need in the workforce to make you happy.

House

Our house is our castle, but we can take it for granted over time. Maybe you are tired of seeing the same thing day after day. If you wish to remain in that home, make some improvements. New windows, new curtains, and even new paint can undoubtedly change the look of it. Add some stunning paintings to create different focal points in each space.

If your home is too big or too expensive, consider selling it and downsizing. Moving to a smaller house can mean less upkeep and it can save you money. Of course you may have to get rid of many goods too so you need to think about what you would be prepared to part with.

Don't get upset if someone owns a bigger home than you do. Don't be angry because it is in a better location than where yours is. Be proud of what you are in and make sure you don't overextend what you can afford to keep up with others you know and their homes.

<h2 align="center"><u>Car</u></h2>

Safety and cost should be significant factors when it comes to buying or leasing an automobile. Don't get one solely to compete with what your neighbours have in the driveway. A sports car isn't going to make you happy, even though it can look snappy and be enjoyable to drive!

<h2 align="center"><u>Children</u></h2>

Don't compare your children to those of someone else! We all have concerns about our kids. Each child has a distinct rate of learning, various interests, and different behaviours. You can't compare what your youngster performs in terms of learning or achievements to others. Focus on what your child offers and that is what will keep you happy as well as them!

<h2 align="center"><u>Appearance</u></h2>

You have to be content with your appearance in order to be happy. You don't have to look like a model though. We regularly see celebrities that look beautiful just a few weeks after giving birth. Keep in mind, they have personal trainers and chefs. They also get help with the baby so they can get proper rest. Someone selects their dress, does their hair, does their makeup.

The average person doesn't have access to those items. Yet we prefer to compare ourselves to the looks of superstars. It is acceptable to idolise celebrities but make sure you keep in mind that they aren't doing it all on their own.

Don't compare your looks to those of your friends or relatives either. We all have unique features that work for us. If you don't like something about your body, work to change them. For example, shed some weight or tone up. If you aren't content with the way your face looks, consider various makeup items. Changing your hair colour and hair cut can also make a difference in how you look.

Be happy with the person you see in the mirror. While we do live in a world that places a tremendous effect on physical appearance, it really is the person inside that will get noticed. If individuals are simply paying attention to you due to physical attributes, those aren't the proper types of people to associate with.

Chapter 8

FACE YOUR FEARS

Nothing will kill happiness or hinder you from obtaining it like dread. There are numerous sorts of fear that people experience that might hold them back. The fear of failing is the biggest one. As we touched on previously, if you don't try then you will never know. Mistakes can happen but so can success.

It might frequently take many trials, errors, and mistakes to be able to reach success. Some of the most successful persons in the world were previously in severe straits due to not giving up on their ideas. With each setback, they learnt one more method not to do what they were trying to achieve.

Being positive and moving through fear is incredibly essential. Think about the best case scenario that can arise from your efforts. Think about the worst case situation too. Be ready for the best but prepare for the worse.

The strange thing about our anxieties is that they are usually not as horrible as the monster we had built in our own minds. When we face those anxieties, we feel empowered and we go forward. We are able to state that we are strong and it provides us a sense of happiness also.

Doubt

Always think that you can do what you set out to do. If you don't have confidence in yourself, you are going to cave in to doubt. If you have positive people around you, they can aid you to erase such doubt. If your social structure consists of individuals that pull you down rather than lifting you up, doubt will win.

When you have doubts, convince yourself why you CAN do what you would like to. Keep in mind that you will always fail if you say nothing or you take no action. It is only when you take actions to go forward that you are able to actually see the difference. If you have doubts, write a list of them. Then write a list of what is at stake for you to gain. Seeing it all on paper can give you the edge you need to take action.

<u>Calculated Risk</u>

Facing concerns though doesn't mean you toss caution to the wind. Some forms of worries actually keep us protected from harm. Think about what you are going to do and why you want to try it. You have nothing to prove to anyone but yourself. Don't allow unsafe pranks to be part of overcoming your anxieties as they could bring you physical injury.

A calculated risk involves looking at the possibilities and coming up with the best appropriate answer for your needs. It helps to look at the common mistakes and ways to prevent them. With this form of risk, you can greatly lower the risk of failure.

<u>Stay Positive</u>

If you are hopeful, you can even gain some amazing energy from your anxieties. Any time that they start to feel bad, spin them around. When you have optimistic thinking, you will attract the success you genuinely want. Focus on breathing regularly when you sense fear so that it won't keep you down.

Focus on successes you have accomplished to help you stay cheerful. If you have just obtained part of your goal, you are still further than when you first began. Don't let failure be all or nothing in your book.

<u>Realistic</u>

You don't want to set yourself up for failure either. You need a realistic plan of action that isn't too difficult or too easy. For example, your objective can't be to lose 25 pounds but you don't plan to modify how you eat or to exercise. You may wish to pursue a better job but you have to realistically be willing to learn some new abilities if you want a better job.

In the next chapter, we will speak about a plan of action and how to use it to move forward in your life. As you do so, you will sense achievement, self worth, and you will be happier!

In the end, we tend to truly only regret the opportunities we didn't take. That is why you have to face your fears and move forward. It isn't always going to be simple, and it won't always work out the way you want it to. Yet you

won't stay awake at night wishing you hadn't
let such a chance pass you by.

Chapter 9

MAKE A PLAN FOR CHANGE

If you can't accept what you have in your life and be content with it, then you need to establish a plan for a change. There can be numerous forms of adjustments that occur to make you happier. Take an inventory of what you need in order to obtain ultimate happiness.

Maybe you need to enhance ties with your family and friends. Maybe you need more time for yourself and for your hobbies. Less stress about money can enable you to be happier. Accepting yourself and being positive can also be part of the plan for improvement.

Time

One of the largest impediments for transformation is time. People feel that they just don't have enough of it. By saying no as talked about in a previous chapter, you can open up time. Start to carve out that period of rest time on your monthly calendar before you fill it up with everything else.

In order for change to occur, you have to be willing to welcome it. Change isn't going to happen lightly, and it can require time and patience. You need a plan of action to help you get there. For example, if you want to become more active, make a schedule that permits you to exercise 30 minutes a day. If the day tends to get away from you, block out time first thing in the morning. If you feel lethargic in the morning though, the afternoon may be a better option.

<u>Enjoyable</u>

Next, pick activities that you enjoy so that you won't try to get out of it. Exercise ought to be something you look forward to rather than trying to avoid. When it comes to change, you won't always get to take part in activities you prefer. That is where discipline comes into the picture.

When that is the case, think about how joyful it is going to be when you do make those changes. Visualise the level of happiness it will give you to stop smoking or to earn your degree. That will enable you to be motivated and to move forward with the necessary duties.

Support

Get encouragement and support from family and friends. Let them know what you wish to alter and why. If you surround yourself with excellent people, they will encourage you and be happy with your accomplishments. This support also binds you to a higher level of accountability than before.

You may find that you get a buddy to help you make the adjustment too. For example, your spouse may decide they will stop smoking or they will make diet and fitness improvements along with you. It really is easier to do anything like that with someone than on your own!

Rewards

Finally, have a means to track your progress and reward your efforts. If you are constantly working out day after day, treat yourself to something such as a new CD or a night at the movies.

You want the rewards to be congruent with what you have in place towards your final aim. For example, if you are going to complete a four year degree, a prize at the conclusion of each completed semester is a fantastic idea. However, you should have a pretty hefty reward waiting for yourself come graduation day!

Resources

Keep in mind that you don't have to take care of everything on your own. There are resources out there to aid you with your plans for transformation. If you want to feel better, consult with your doctor. If you want to eat healthier, sit down with a dietitian. A financial planner can help you with budgeting and with retirement. Use the resources that make it easy for you to have a clear path to your goals.

Write It Down

Your plan of action for change and a happier you should be written down. This makes it more tangible. Have a start date and an end date for accomplishing your ultimate goal. If the goal is broad and long term, break it down so you have mini stages to complete along the way. Being able to celebrate that success will keep you motivated.

<u>Evaluate</u>

At regular intervals, evaluate your plan of action for change. Are you happier? Do you feel the plan is still working for you? If not, redesign it. You may find that altering key components of your plan help you to move beyond any problems that you didn't foresee along your journey

Chapter 10

TAKE CARE OF YOUR MIND AND BODY

If you want to be happy in life, you need to take care of your mind and your body. The mind and body function in harmony with each other thus they should be able to deliver you the very best. When they aren't in sync but you have to make an effort to get them back to that place.

Chemicals in the Brain

In order to experience happiness, there are particular chemicals in the brain that must be present. The chemical equilibrium of the brain is exceedingly complex. Taking part in exercise will aid to release feel good hormones. Some individuals don't have the correct combination of molecules that they need.

If that may be the situation, drugs may be important to help control them. Many people suffer from mental health difficulties including depression that prohibit them from being as joyful as they would like to be. Talk to a professional about the potential and see if they can enable you to be happier than you thought imaginable. If all your efforts alone don't improve that level, this may be the next step to consider.

Lifestyle Habits

The mind needs to relax just like the body does. Getting adequate sleep each night is important for the mind and the body. It will offer you extra energy and allow you to be alert. When the intellect is sharp, you get more completed in less time. You can also be more inventive.

Avoid undesirable habits including drinking excessively, taking illegal drugs, and smoking. They can all contribute to major health concerns. It can be hard to stop using such products owing to the physical and emotional addiction to them. However, there are tools out there that may help offer solutions so you don't have to feel alone with your efforts.

Eat Well

Your mind and your body benefit from eating healthy. Your body and brain get enough from the foods you ingest. When you eat foods that are abundant in antioxidants, it delivers a boost for the immune system. This includes fresh fruits and vegetables.

Your body and brain require enough protein also in order to help with energy. When you consume foods that are high in processed carbs or sweets, it can diminish your feeling of happiness. It can cause the brain to get smaller and increase the risk of depression.

Checkups

Routine exams for your medical needs, dental care, and vision are also crucial. Such exams should be arranged annually. Don't wait until you have a concern to take action. If you have a family history of health issues, be sure your doctor is aware of them. Early testing can play a role in prevention.

Regular checkups can help with early action if a problem is discovered. It can make a tremendous impact in the forms of treatment that are available for the health care need. It can also indicate the difference between the need for continued treatment or a one time remedy.

Pay Attention

Don't disregard any warnings from your head or your body that something isn't right. If you are feeling anything that is strange, take action. Too many people overlook it because they are terrified or they don't have the time to deal with it. Yet those early warning indicators can avert problems that can't be reversed later on.

Be proactive when it comes to taking care of your mind, your body, and your general well-being. It is a crucial step towards feeling fantastic and towards being joyful.

CONCLUSION

Are you happy? Maybe you think you are happy enough? Perhaps you have been miserable for so long that it seems like just a part of life. Now is the moment to switch things up and see what materialises. Don't let fear of the unknown or fear of failure hold you back.

Don't be so anxious about what others think. As long as your attempts to be joyful don't affect anyone else, then keep your head up and confidently take part in them. Do what you can to keep money striving from affecting your degree of enjoyment. Worrying about money might make it hard to be happy about much else.

For many people, just finding the fortitude to say no to several time draining activities is a significant step forward. They feel more in charge of the day. They appreciate seeing some blank areas on the calendar rather than every single time slot filled in. They prefer having time to do nothing or time to visit with someone they love.

What will people say about you when it is time for your funeral services? Hopefully, they will be able to say you were fun, cheerful, and lived your life to the fullest every single day. You have the choice to be happy so you can start to shift things around or leave them precisely as they are right now. If your self-esteem is poor, you need to fix it. If you are often not feeling well about who you are, it is tough to be joyful.

Don't be so concentrated simply on physical beauty either. It may surprise you exactly how many people out there that are stunning aren't happy. They often wonder if others like them for anything else. The same goes for folks with gobs of money. They usually worry that people just want some cash and not truly anything about them individually.

What this means is that we all have our inner troubles and our outer variables that we have to learn to contend with. The actual world isn't always kind, so make sure you are always good to yourself first. Take time to be kind and kind to individuals in your life as well as strangers on the street. It may make more of a difference to them than you can ever know.

One of the easiest methods to transform your perspective is to take part in a daily activity where you express appreciation. Make a list of a few things you are grateful for and start your day off with happy thoughts. It can actually impact the way that your entire day plays out.

As soon as you realise it isn't about materials items and money, you can discover happiness. It gets difficult and harder for the younger generations to get that message. We live in a world that seems to encourage material items as the key to a happy existence. So much of the advertising out there shows this. They never show someone in an older automobile that is paid for smiling and pleased. They want you to think you need a new car and the payment that goes along with it!

While we don't have control over everything that happens around us, we do have the choice to be happy. People who are happy and successful in life aren't just lucky. Instead, they cherish the tiny things and they surround themselves with people who are optimistic.

They make time for themselves so that they aren't overloaded. They take time to unwind and to engage in things that are pleasurable for them. They aim to have a healthy body and a healthy mind so that they can continue to feel happy at any age.

Identify what true happiness means to you, and then do all you can to make it happen. You have some very good information from this content to assist you make great changes that will affect your life for the better. Pick one adjustment to make at a time and really focus on it.

As you do well with it, add another to the mix. You will notice that you start to feel happier in no time at all. Stop spending your time on hobbies and people that bring you down. Life is simply too brief to be anything but happy.